Taking Down Syndrome to School

by Jenna Glatzer

Adapted for the Special Kids in School® series
created by Kim Gosselin

JayJo Books, L.L.C.
Publishing Special Books for Special Kids®

Taking Down Syndrome to School
© 2002 JayJo Books, LLC
Edited by Karen Schader

Published by
JayJo Books, LLC
A Guidance Channel Company
Publishing Special Books for Special Kids®

JayJo Books is a publisher of books to help teachers, parents, and children cope with chronic illnesses, special needs, and health education in classroom, family, and social settings.

Library of Congress Control Number: 2001098366
ISBN 1-891383-19-1
First Edition
Twelfth book in our *Special Kids in School*® series

For information about
Premium and Special Sales, contact:
JayJo Books Special Sales Office
P.O. Box 213
Valley Park, MO 63088-0213
636-861-1331
jayjobooks@aol.com
www.jayjo.com

For all other information, contact:
JayJo Books
135 Dupont Street, P.O. Box 760
Plainview, NY 11803-0760
1-800-999-6884
jayjobooks@guidancechannel.com
www.jayjo.com

Dedication

For Alex Saladino, Stevie Zacharias, Katie Atkinson,
everyone at Unomas21.com, and all of the other kids and angels
with Down syndrome.

Note from the Author

My 22-year old brother, Paul Glatzer, has Down syndrome. I didn't have to dedicate this book to him, because he already knows he's my favorite person in the world.

Paul has been very lucky that, all through his life, people have loved him and included him. But one day, he came to me and wanted to know what the word "retard" meant. That's when I knew books like this one would be important to me. Now, I frequently write about people with disabilities and the legislation and ethical issues that affect them.

I hope I can help other people understand what's special about people with Down syndrome, and I hope everyone who reads this book will have the opportunity to have their lives touched by someone as wonderful and inspiring as Paul.

You may contact the author at jenna@absolutewrite.com.

Hi! My name is Nick, and I have Down syndrome. I was born with Down syndrome (or "DS" for short), and I will have it for the rest of my life. Some things about me are different from you. But if you get to know me, you'll find out we have lots of things in common.

I love chocolate ice cream. Is that your favorite too?

Some kids with DS go to special schools, but not me. I go to a public school with all sorts of kids. Some have disabilities like me, but most of them don't.

I think it's great that we all get to meet each other and learn from each other!

I started going to school when I was just a baby. My doctor told my mom it was a good idea to get me started at school early so I could get a head start. One thing you might notice about me is that I don't learn as fast as you do. I have to work extra hard to understand things in school.

I am working super hard on my reading right now, because I want to read all the same books that you can read!

There are other things that are hard for me too. Sometimes I stutter or don't speak very clearly. Mrs. Randall, a special kind of teacher called a "speech therapist," helps me exercise the muscles in my mouth. We practice the sounds of letters and words. You may have trouble understanding what I say. If you do, just ask me to say it again. You can ask my teacher to help too.

It really helps me if you take time to try and understand me!

Not all kids with DS are the same. Some of them have more trouble learning than I do. I am lucky because I am learning handwriting and math. Some kids with DS can't do that.

Sometimes, kids with DS have other problems with their health. When I was just a baby, there was a tiny hole inside my heart. I had an operation to patch up the hole. Now I'm good as new!

Good thing my mom met some smart doctors!

I also look a little different than you. Most people with DS are short, like me. I don't mind being short though. It means I can find more places to hide when we play Hide 'n Seek!

I also have short, stubby fingers. My eyes are slanted too. My mom says that when I smile, you can barely see my eyes at all! I like to smile a lot.

I hope she won't forget what color my eyes are!

You can't catch DS from me or anyone else. Either you are born with it, or you aren't. It's not a sickness, like a cold or flu. So it's okay to play with me! In fact, I would love playing with you. I like having fun, just like you do.

My friends are very important to me.

I like to play sports, even though I may not be the best player on the team. It's important for me to exercise and build strong muscles. My muscles have a little trouble learning too! They don't grow as fast as yours. Usually I have to work harder to control them.

Did you know your tongue is a muscle? When I was younger, I had trouble making my tongue do what I wanted it to do. Sometimes it looked like I was sticking my tongue out at people even when I didn't mean to. Oops!

I'm glad I don't do that anymore.

In school, I am in a special education class. That's a class for kids who need extra time and extra help to learn. I have a teacher and a teacher's assistant. I like all the kids in my class, and we get to know each other very well.

Sometimes I wish I could meet more kids in other classes too!

Now I have a secret to tell you. There's one thing that really, really hurts my feelings. Usually I don't like to say it out loud. But I'll say it this once, so maybe you can help me. Sometimes, kids call me names, like "stupid" or "dummy." That makes me feel bad. The name that's the very worst of all, though, is "retard." I'm not sure if other kids know what that word really means. "Retard" is short for "retarded," and retarded means slow. But when kids call me "retard," they say it to make me feel bad.

Please don't make fun of me because I have DS. If you call me names, it makes me feel like you think I'm stupid. I work very hard to try to be as smart as you are.

I hope if you hear someone use the word "retard," you'll tell them to stop.

There is no cure for Down syndrome, so I will always have it. You don't have to feel bad for me, though. DS is just a part of who I am. I don't like it though when kids make fun of me. I'd much rather be your friend!

If you see me, please say "hi" and get to know me better. You might just find out that I'm a lot of fun!

And I could always use another friend ... couldn't you?

DOWN SYNDROME KiDS' QUiZ!

1. How should you treat a person with Down syndrome?

I hope you will treat me just like any other kid!

2. What causes Down syndrome?

Everyone who has Down syndrome was born with an extra chromosome.

3. Why do some people with Down syndrome look like they're sticking out their tongues?

It's harder for us to control our muscles. When our tongue muscle is relaxed, it likes to "hang out." We do mouth exercises to help this.

4. What does "retarded" mean?

It means "slow." When someone says I am "mentally retarded," it just means I learn slowly.

5. Can you catch Down syndrome from me?

No. If you weren't born with it like I was, you will never get it. It is not contagious. I can't give you Down syndrome.

6. Does everyone in my family have DS?

No. I'm the only one. My mom, dad, and sister don't have Down syndrome.

7. What should you do if you don't understand what I'm saying?

You can ask me to say it again, or you can ask a teacher to help us understand each other better.

8. What is a special education class?

It's a class for kids who need extra time and extra help to learn, like me. Our teachers take more time to explain what we need to learn. They want to make sure we understand everything.

9. Why does it hurt my feelings when people call me names?

I have feelings just like you. It makes me sad when people make fun of me. I didn't do anything wrong to get Down syndrome and it's nobody's fault. I don't like to feel different from other kids.

10. Is there a cure for Down syndrome?

No. There's no medicine I can take to make my DS go away. I will have it for the rest of my life.

11. If someone else is making fun of me, what should you say?

It would be very nice if you would tell them you don't think it's funny. I have feelings just like everyone else. It's not nice to hurt people's feelings just because they're different. After all, everyone is different in some way!

Great job! Thanks for taking the Down Syndrome Kids' Quiz!

TEN TIPS FOR TEACHERS

✔ **1. WHEN YOU DON'T UNDERSTAND, ASK.**
If a person with DS is stuttering or having trouble "getting the words out," ask him or her to slow down, think about what he or she is trying to say, and then try again.

✔ **2. IF THAT FAILS, MOVE ON.**
It can be very frustrating for a person with DS to keep repeating something without being understood. If you're not getting anywhere, forget about it and move the conversation to something else.

✔ **3. WATCH FOR OVER-AFFECTIONATE BEHAVIOR.**
Kids with DS can be very physically affectionate to everyone from their classmates to bus drivers to strangers! Try to explain why this may be inappropriate without discouraging the good feelings behind it. Offer other ways to show their feelings.

✔ **4. EDUCATE THE NAME-CALLERS.**
If you hear someone use the word "retard" in your class, don't just scold. Explain what the word really means, and why it's hurtful to people with disabilities.

✔ **5. USE 'PEOPLE FIRST' LANGUAGE.**
Remember, it's not a "Down syndrome boy," but rather, a boy living with Down syndrome. The same applies to other disabilities. Be sure the person comes BEFORE the handicap (i.e., "a boy in a wheelchair" instead of "a wheelchair-bound boy," or "a teenager who is blind" instead of "a blind teenager").

6. ENCOURAGE INTERACTION.

Help your students interact with kids with Down syndrome whenever possible! If you notice a "special education table" at the cafeteria, ask your students if they'd like to take turns making some new friends.

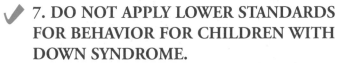

7. DO NOT APPLY LOWER STANDARDS FOR BEHAVIOR FOR CHILDREN WITH DOWN SYNDROME.

If a person with DS is misbehaving, treat him or her just as you would any other student. It's important for them to learn appropriate manners and behavior too!

8. EXPLAIN DS IS NOT CONTAGIOUS.

Reassure students that people with DS are not "sick." Remind them that no one can catch DS from them or anyone else.

9. EACH CHILD WITH DS IS UNIQUE.

Kids with DS have a wide range of learning capabilities and health conditions. Many have heart and digestive disorders, while others are perfectly healthy. Check with the student's parents about diet or exercise restrictions.

10. EMPHASIZE THE STRENGTHS OF THE CHILD LIVING WITH DS.

Is the child cheerful or friendly? Is he or she a good artist or really funny? A great dancer or a loyal friend? Help the other kids to recognize the positives in kids living with DS. The most important gift you can give to people with disabilities is making them feel included. Just like everyone else, they want to be liked and appreciated for exactly who they are!

ADDITIONAL RESOURCES

**Association for Children
With Down Syndrome**
4 Fern Place
Plainview, NY 11803
(516) 933-4700
http://www.acds.org/

Best Buddies
100 Southeast Second Street, Suite 1990
Miami, Florida 33131
(305) 374-2233
http://www.bestbuddies.org

Down Syndrome: Health Issues
http://www.ds-health.com/

DownsCity
http://www.downscity.com/

National Down Syndrome Congress
7000 Peachtree-Dunwoody Road, N.E.
Lake Ridge 400 Office Park Building #5,
Suite 100
Atlanta, GA 30328-1655
(800) 232-NDSC
http://www.ndsccenter.org

National Down Syndrome Society
666 Broadway
New York, NY 10012
(212) 460-9330
http://www.ndss.org

Uno Mas!
P.O. Box 372
Murrieta, CA 92564
http://www.unomas21.com

To order additional copies of *Taking Down Syndrome to School* or inquire about our quantity discounts for schools, hospitals, and affiliated organizations, contact us at 1-800-999-6884.

From our *Special Kids in School*® series
Taking A.D.D. to School
Taking Asthma to School
Taking Autism to School
Taking Cancer to School
Taking Cerebral Palsy to School
Taking Cystic Fibrosis to School
Taking Diabetes to School
Taking Dyslexia to School
Taking Food Allergies to School
Taking Seizure Disorders to School
Taking Tourette Syndrome to School
...and others coming soon!

From our new *Healthy Habits for Kids*® series
There's a Louse in My House
A Fun Story about Kids and Head Lice

From our new *Special Family and Friends*™ series
Allie Learns About Alzheimer's Disease
A Family Story about Love, Patience, and Acceptance
Patrick Learns About Parkinson's Disease
A Story of a Special Bond Between Friends
... and others coming soon!

And from our *Substance Free Kids*® series
Smoking STINKS!!™
A Heartwarming Story about the Importance of Avoiding Tobacco

Other books available now!
SPORTSercise!
A School Story about
Exercise-Induced Asthma
ZooAllergy
A Fun Story about Allergy
and Asthma Triggers
Rufus Comes Home
Rufus the Bear with Diabetes™
A Story about Diagnosis and Acceptance
The ABC's of Asthma
An Asthma Alphabet Book
for Kids of All Ages
Taming the Diabetes Dragon
A Story about Living Better
with Diabetes
Trick-or-Treat for Diabetes
A Halloween Story for Kids
Living with Diabetes

A portion of the proceeds from all our publications is donated to various charities to help fund important medical research and education. We work hard to make a difference in the lives of children with chronic conditions and/or special needs. Thank you for your support.